ARCO-AIRCAM AVIATION SERIES **No. 19**

F–86A Sabre, 56th Fighter Group, O'Hare Air Force Bas
Eater'. Natural metal scheme, yellow trim with black outline

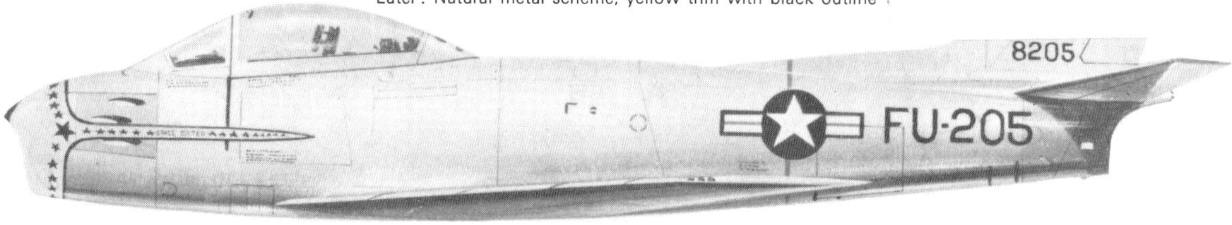

NORTH AMERICAN F-86A-L SABRE
IN USAF & FOREIGN SERVICE

Illustrated and compiled by
Richard Ward

Text by
Ernest R. McDowell

ACKNOWLEDGEMENTS

This book on the North American F–86 Sabre is the first of two titles in the AIRCAM AVIATION SERIES covering the type; the second book will deal with Canadair and Commonwealth Aircraft Sabres. The Sabre has been built in larger numbers and flown by more of the air forces of the West than any other type of jet fighter; it still flies as first line equipment of many air forces and no doubt will continue to do so for a long time in the future. My thanks to all those who assisted with photographs and information, whose names are listed below in alphabetical order.
R. A. Brown, G. Cattaneo, J. C. Cuny, C. R. Elliot, T. G. Handelman, R. W. Harrison, Maj. A. P. de Jong, G. Joos, G. H. Kamphuis, W. T. Larkins, G. J. Letzter, E. R. McDowell, D. W. Menard, S. P. Peltz, T. Shibusawa, J. Stoppel, N. E. Taylor, G. C. Voldonio, RAF, RNethAF, RNorAF, SAAF, French AF, Italian AF, USAF.

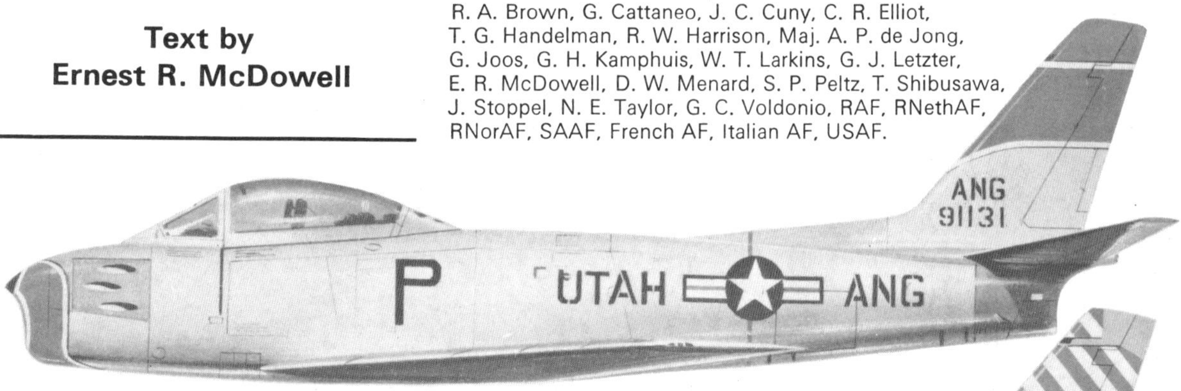

F–86A Sabre, Utah Air National Guard. Green trim outlined white and black, natural metal scheme.

F–86E Sabre, unit unknown, Dayton AFB, Ohio, September 1955. Natural metal finish with pale blue and white trim.

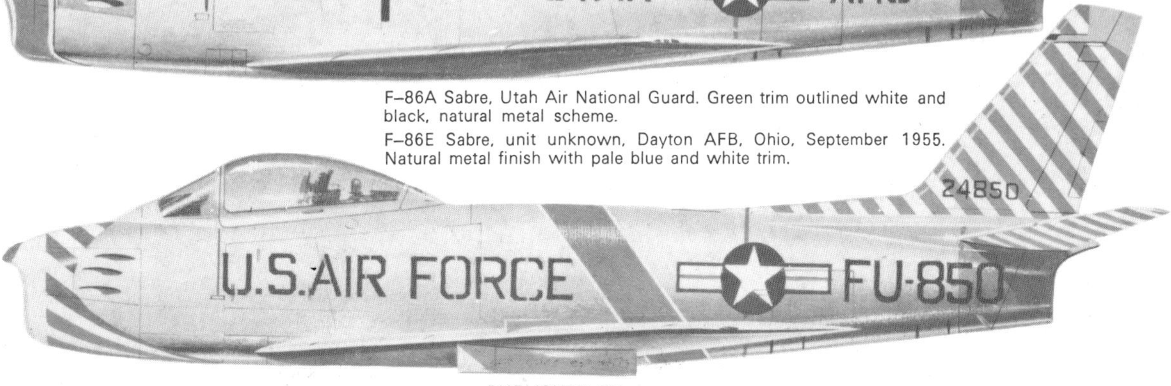

PUBLISHED BY
Arco Publishing Company, Inc., 219 Park Avenue South, New York, N.Y. 10003
First Published by Osprey Publications Ltd., and Printed in Great Britain
Library of Congress No. 79-113953 · Library Edition SBN 668-02300-7 · Paperback Edition SBN 668-02301-5

Above: Neat formation of F–86K's by No. 700 Squadron, Royal Netherlands Air Force. Note the early formal presentation of the squadron insignia. (Royal Netherlands Air Force)

Below: Another neat formation this time by F–86D's of the 56th Fighter Interceptor Wing, 63rd Fighter Interceptor Squadron, Wurtsmith Air Force Base, Michigan 1964. (USAF)

Formation of 51st Fighter Wing Sabres over Korea, an E–10 leading a couple of E–5's with a Canadair built E–6 in the slot. See colour illustration. (USAF)

NORTH AMERICAN F-86A-L SABRE

North American Aviation, after producing the outstanding American fighter of World War II in its P-51 Mustang, followed up this success when it entered the jet propulsion field and turned out the F-86 Sabre, which went on to become the best fighter of the Korean conflict.

Like the P-51, which owed its existence to the R.A.F., the F-86 likewise owed its design to another service, in this case the U.S. Navy. North America's first jet design (NA-134) which had begun in the fall of 1944 was intended to be a carrier fighter. The Navy placed an order for three prototypes of the XFJ-1 on 1st January, 1945. This was the first order that North American had ever received from the Navy for a fighter.

A design study was initiated on 22nd November, 1944 (as RD-1265), by North American with the goal of producing a new design based on the NA-134 which would interest the Air Force. It was hoped that the elimination of the specialized equipment required by the Navy might improve performances enough to attract Air Force interest. This design, the NA-140, resulted in an order for three prototype aircraft to be designated the XP-86 by the Air Force.

The XP-86 Prototype

Since the XP-86 was to be a land-based fighter, North American was able to use a much thinner wing and a narrower fuselage. This resulted in the extension of the critical Mach number from 0.8 on the FJ-1 to 0.9 on the XP-86.

The design was straightforward, with a low, straight wing and tail planes and a nose air intake and the usual tricycle landing gear. Wing span was 38.2 feet, length 35.5 feet and height 13.2 feet. Combat radius was 297 miles with a service ceiling of 46,000 feet. The plane grossed out at 11,500 pounds, and top speeds of 574 m.p.h. at sea level and 582 m.p.h. at 10,000 feet were anticipated.

The wind tunnel results indicated that the XP-86 would not be able to attain the anticipated 600 m.p.h. that the Air Force demanded, and would not even be able to equal the speed of the Republic F-84. This seemed to be the end of the line for the F-86 design.

Project aerodynamicist L. P. Greene and his team now turned to the swept-back wing as data from captured German documents seemed to indicate that sweeping back the wing delayed and reduced the drag rise and offered great promise in highspeed flight. Swept wings produced certain undesirable stability effects which had to be overcome before the wing could be used on production fighters. German tests with a leading edge slat gave promising information on the low speed stability problem. The answer seemed to rest in the ability to develop an automatically operated slat, one completely independent of pilot control. Wind tunnel testing suggested that this could be the answer and a new design study, RD-1369, was submitted to the Air Force and was approved on 1st November, 1945.

The wing design finally adopted called for a 35 degree sweep-back, an aspect ratio of 4.79 and a thickness/chord ratio of 11% at the wing root and 10% at the wing tip. Wing leading edge slats were designed to open automatically and fully at 130 knots, and to close automatically and fully at 290 knots IAS; later these were changed to 115 and 180 knots respectively, beginning with the 160th F-86A.

The prototype, serial number 45-59597, was completed on 8th August and on 1st October North American test pilot George Welch took the XP-86 into the air on its maiden flight. Welch was a fighter ace who had scored 16 kills, and was one of the pilots who shot down Japanese aircraft during the attack on Pearl Harbour. What was to have been a short routine familiarization flight almost turned into a disaster when the nose wheel jammed part way down upon being lowered for the landing. After efforts failed to free it, Welch brought the aircraft in with the nose high. The jolt of the main gear hitting the runway freed the nose wheel, and it held for the roll-out, enabling Welch to bring the XP-86 to a safe stop.

Testing consisted of three phases; Phase I was completed after 30 hours of flying without further incident, and the aircraft was turned over to the Air Force for

Phase II. These tests were flown by Major Ken Chilstrom, who logged a mere 10 hours and 17 minutes, making a total of 11 hops to complete the testing in a week's time. Phase III was the real test of the bird and several months were necessary to conduct the many operations scheduled. On 26th April, 1948, the prototype exceeded Mach One for the first time in a shallow dive with Welch at the controls, becoming the first combat aircraft in the Western world to exceed the speed of sound. The prototype was officially delivered on 30th November, 1948, and was destroyed in a crash in September of 1952. The second and third prototypes were flown for 202 and 75 hours respectively. They were withdrawn from service in 1953.

Production Sabres

The Air Force had contracted for 33 P-86A's on 20th December, 1946, and a fixed price contract was authorized for these 33 on 16th October, 1947. A supplement to this contract authorized the purchase of 190 F-86B's. North American proposed to substitute 188 F-86A's plus two F-86C's on 1st December, 1947, and this was accepted by the Air Force, who issued a contract change notice on 16th December to cover it and to discontinue the F-86B.

The F-86A was powered first by the General Electric J-47-GE-7 and later by the J-47-GE-13. Wing span was 37.12 feet, length 37.54 feet and height 14.74 feet. Combat radius was 330 miles, service ceiling 48,000 feet, speed 679 m.p.h. at sea level and 601 m.p.h. at 35,000 feet. Combat weight figured out at 13,791 pounds.

As we have seen the F-86B was cancelled. The F-86C was such a radical departure from the basic design that it was initially designated the F-93A. The nose intake was changed to two flush intakes on the sides of the fuselage and power was furnished by the XJ-48-P-3. Top speed was increased to 709 m.p.h. Span increased to 38 feet 9 inches, length to 44 feet 1 inch and height to 15 feet 8 inches. Service ceiling decreased to 46,800 feet but speed at 35,000 had increased to 622 m.p.h. George Welch was at the controls when it made its first flight on 25th January, 1950. The C-model was to have been a long range fighter, but only two were procured. Radar had been installed in the nose and the main gear consisted of twin wheels. The aircraft was not a success and the 118 production models ordered were cancelled even before the prototype had flown. The F-86D, the famed "Sabre Dog", was originally conceived as a night fighter and given the designation F-95, but was redesignated as the D in July of 1950. This model involved about a 75% redesign of the F-86A. The radar was housed in a radome mounted on the nose above the air intake opening; the nose gave this version a distinctive profile. A retractable rack was installed in the belly to carry twenty-four 2.75 rockets. These were the FFAR "Mickey Mouse" type with a 7.55 pound warhead. They could be fired in groups or salvoed. The Hughes E-3 and later E-4 fire control systems were installed. Other changes included a clam shell canopy with a rearward hinge, all-flying tail plane, hydraulic controls, and afterburner for the J47-GE-17 engine.

First flight took place on 22nd December, 1949, with George Welch at the controls. On 18th November, 1952, Capt. J. S. Nash broke the speed record set by an F-86A in 1948 with a speed of 698.505 m.p.h., flying a Sabre Dog. This record fell to another F-86D on 16th July, 1953, flown by Lt.-Col. Bill Barnes, whose speed was 715.697 m.p.h.

Changes continued to be made and are too numerous to cover fully in this text. Some important ones were as follows: the F-86D-10 was equipped with a powered rudder without a trim tab; the D-15 incorporated a single point refuelling station; the D-20 had a fuel filter de-icing system added; and the D-25 was modified to carry 120 gallon drop tanks on long combat missions rather than just on ferry trips.

The F-86E was identical to the A-model except for the all-flying tail plane which was later used on the D-model.

PU–608 an F–86A flown by Maj. R. L. Johnson in an abortive attempt to break the world's speed record during the National Air Races at Cleveland, Ohio, September 1948. Note red tail unit and outer wing panels, control surfaces natural metal. (D. W. Menard)

The E's elevators and horizontal stabilizer were controlled and operated as a single unit. The stabilizer was pivoted around its rear spar so that the leading edge had an eight degree travel up and down which could be controlled by normal control column movements. The elevators were linked mechanically to the stabilizer and moved in a specific relationship to its movement. The elevator travel was slightly greater than the stabilizer movement.

The new systems eliminated a number of control problems and gave more positive action. Trim tabs were eliminated and the controls were irreversible, but an artificial "feel" had to be provided for the pilot to give the normal feel to the controls.

The F-86F was basically a modification to the E-model to take the newer and more powerful J47-GE-27 engine, although a few other changes were incorporated in the F series, such as a flat wind shield on the dash 10, and larger wing shackles and strengthened hard points to accept a 200 gallon drop tank on the dash 5; this increased the range to a radius of 463 miles. The dash 10 also got a new gunsight, the A-4, which was simpler and easier to maintain than the A-1CM used on the A and E models. The F-86FR had Sidewinder missile capability added.

The F-86G was produced in limited quantity; 16 in all were turned out with the J47-GE-29 engine.

The F-86H was designed to accept the GE-J-73 engine and serve as a fighter-bomber. The fuselage was six inches deeper to provide the enlarged air intake demanded by the J-73. Wing fences were incorporated on the dash 5 model. The F-86H added the atomic bomb capability to the Sabre series, provision being made to carry the 1,200 pound tactical nuclear weapon under the port wing with drop tanks under the starboard wing as a counterbalance. A low altitude bombing system device was installed which enabled the pilot to "lob" the bomb, make an Immelmann turn and escape the blast. Capt. Joe McConnell was killed on 26th August, 1954, while flying a test on the F-86H; he was the top ace of the Korean War.

The letters I and J were not assigned. The F-86K was basically a Sabre Dog intended for the NATO nations under the Mutual Security Program. It was equipped with a simpler weapons system consisting of four 20 mm. M-39 guns and the MG-4 fire control system. The K was slightly longer than the D model.

The last of the series, the F-86L was simply an updated Sabre Dog which was modernized by extending the wing tips two feet, adding a slotted wing leading edge and the "Data Link" black boxes which received data from SAGE's ground computer and direct the pilot's instruments accordingly until he makes the interception.

A two-seater trainer version was produced in the TF-86, but it was unsuccessful; only two were built and the first crashed on 17th March, 1954, killing another test pilot, Joseph Lynch. Later that year George Welch was killed testing the F-100, the new Super Sabre.

Several attempts were made to produce a reconnais-

Above & left: The first Sabres to cross the Atlantic were these of the 116th Fighter Squadron which arrived at Shepherds Grove, Suffolk, UK, on 27th August 1951. The squadron was the first USAF unit stationed in the UK since WWII. Red trim, outlined with black on fuselage, black and white 'Ace of Clubs' insignia. (Top, C. R. Elliot; lower RAF)

sance version by field modifications and a limited number were converted as RF-86A's carrying a 24 inch K-22 dicing camera and two 20 inch K-24's. Later several F-86F-30's were modified as RF-86F's with two K-22 and one K-17 cameras fitted. Seven of these were sent to the Chinese Nationalists.

The Sabre Jet in Combat

The entry of Communist China into the Korean conflict resulted in the appearance of the Russian-built MiG 15 in the skies over the Yalu. At one fell stroke all U.N. fighter aircraft were rendered obsolete; they simply could not cope with the ceiling and speed of the MiG 15.

In an attempt to equalize matters the U.S.A.F. hurriedly ordered two jet wings to the Far East. These were the F-84-equipped 27th Wing and the F-86A-equipped 4th Fighter Wing. Departing the U.S.A. in the middle of November, the 4th Fighter-Interceptor Wing took off from Kimpo on an orientation flight on 15th December. The Sabres had arrived and were ready. Two days later, 17th December, 1950, the 4th took off again — and this time the mission was a combat sortie. Their baptism of fire wasn't long in coming. Lt.-Col. Bruce Hinton and his flight spotted a flight of four MiGs. Although the Sabre pilots were moving at only 0.62 Mach to conserve fuel they batted their throttles full out and were on the startled MiGs very quickly. Apparently the MiG pilots and enemy radar had mistaken them for the slower F-80s. Col. Hinton and his wing man cut off a MiG from the sanctuary of the Yalu and Hinton snapped off several long bursts which caught the MiG in a vital spot, causing it to burst into flames and slowly spin in and crash. Col. Hinton thus became the first Sabre pilot to register a victory.

The next few days brought about a change in tactics on the part of the Sabre pilots. They dropped the idea of a low cruising speed to save fuel, and if MiGs were about they entered the patrol area at speeds of between 0.85 and 0.87 Mach. Although this shortened their patrol time to twenty minutes it soon began to pay off in kills.

On 22nd December eight F-86A's left Kimpo on a patrol. One flight was flying at 35,000 feet at the new higher speed when they were bounced by some MiGs, who dived through their formation, firing as they came and then continued at high speed across the Yalu. Capt. Larry Bach's Sabre was hit and he spun out of the formation in flames, the first Sabre to fall to enemy guns in combat.

When the afternoon patrol of eight Sabres took off they were praying for a chance to even the score. The first flight was led by Lt.-Col. John C. Meyer, the C.O. of the 4th and a Second World War ace with 24 aerial kills to his credit. The second flight was led by Lt.-Col. Glenn T. Eagleston, another ace, with a record of 20½ aerial kills. They soon encountered a formation of fifteen-plus MiGs, and this time the new tactics paid off richly; they " flamed " six MiGs in a running dogfight that lasted twenty minutes and ranged from 30,000 feet right down to the deck.

By the end of December the Sabres had chalked up a total of eight kills, two probables, and seven others damaged against the single loss of Capt. Bach. Flying 234 sorties, they had regained aerial supremacy over Korea for the U.N. forces.

Due to a deterioration in the ground situation the 4th Wing had to be withdrawn from Kimpo on 2nd January, 1951. As the Red advance continued on the ground the Sabre was called upon to perform a new rôle, that of a close support aircraft, in an effort to slow the Communist advance and relieve pressure on the ground troops. Despite the fact that they were not well suited for this rôle the Sabres managed to fly 158 sorties along with 104 armed reconnaissance sorties and eight combat patrols by the end of January.

Early in March, after the ground situation was somewhat improved, Col. Eagleston's 334th Squadron began staging through Suwon Airfield and were joined by the 336th Squadron shortly thereafter, while the 335th was held in reserve in Japan.

Bitter fighting continued both in the air and on the ground, and soon the area along the Yalu River became known as MiG Alley. Victories were scored in the air by both sides, and the leading scorer was Capt. James Jabara, of the 334th, with four kills. The 334th was relieved by the 335th and rotated back to Japan to rest, but Capt. Jabara asked for and received permission to remain in combat. His fourth kill had come on 22nd April and it wasn't until 20th May that he got a chance to score again.

At about 17.00 hours on that day fourteen Sabres of the 4th were jumped by about 50 MiGs over Sinuiju.

F–86A of the 1st Fighter Group, 94th Fighter Squadron, note the 'Hat in the Ring' insignia and 1st FG insignia on fuselage The 94th was the first squadron to receive Sabres. (USAF)

Jabara was in the second wave of fourteen Sabres which bored in to help the first wave. He tacked on to three MiGs at about 35,000 feet, picked the "tail end Charlie" and roared straight in. His first two bursts hit the left wing and fuselage. At about 10,000 feet the pilot baled out just before the MiG exploded. Number five down! But the battle was still on, so Jabara climbed back to 20,000 and bounced six more MiGs. He closed in and snapped off two bursts into one of the six MiGs, scoring heavily with both and causing the MiG to smoke. Another burst caught the enemy square in the middle and the MiG burst into flames and went into an uncontrolled spin. All Jabara could see was a swirl of fire, and he had to break off as another MiG had latched onto his tail. Jabara thus became the first "jet-against-jet" ace in the history of aerial warfare.

On 8th July a squadron of Mustangs was bounced by MiGs, who in turn were jumped by Sabres. Three MiGs were destroyed in the fight. One of these fell before the guns of America's top living ace, Col. Francis S. Gabreski, new deputy C.O. of the 4th. In September Captains Ralph Gibson and Richard Becker joined Jabara in the select circle of jet aces, each bagging their fifth on 9th September, 1951.

Red air activity began to increase and the fighter-bombers were forced out of the front areas along the Yalu. The MiGs then went after the B-29's with their F-84 escorts, and soon forced the mediums to abandon daylight bombing as too costly, despite the efforts of the F-84 and F-86 pilots.

The month of November produced three more jet aces — Lt.-Col. Richard D. Creighton on the 27th and Major George A. Davis and Lt.-Col. Winton W. Marshall on the 30th. Major Davis had a habit of getting his kills like bananas, in bunches; after he scored his first kill, he proceeded to bag four to achieve ace status in a single mission, getting three Tu-2's and a MiG on the 30th November. He got another pair on 5th December, picked up four more on 13th December in a big running fight, and bagged a pair in seconds on his last mission before being shot down and lost on 10th February, 1952. His final total stood at 14; with 11 MiGs and three Tu-2's he was the leading ace at the time of his death. He was awarded the Congressional Medal of Honor posthumously for bravery.

In an attempt to counteract the increasing number of MiGs being committed by the Communist air forces the U.S.A.F. ordered 75 F-86E's to the Far East to be used to re-equip the 51st Wing, which was operating F-80's.

On 2nd November Lt.-Col. George L. Jones shot down the 100th MiG to be destroyed in combat by the U.S.A.F.

The 51st Wing's Sabres became operational on 1st December with Col. Gabreski as Wing Commander and Lt.-Col. George Jones as the group C.O. The 51st got into a scrap with some MiGs on 23rd February, 1952, and the C.O. of the 25th Squadron, Major William T. Whisner, got his fifth MiG to become the first ace from the 51st Wing.

April was a vintage month for new jet aces; Col. Gabreski on the 1st, Capt. Robert H. Moore on the 3rd, Capt. Iven C. Kinchlee on the 6th, Capt. Robert Love on the 21st, and Maj. William Wescott on the 26th all scored victory number five and ran the jet ace list to twelve.

Four more aces were created in May as Maj. Don Adams, Lt. James H. Kasler, Capt. Robert T. Latshaw, Jr., and Col. Harrison R. Thyng all joined the select group. On the minus side Col. Walker H. Mahurin, a high-scoring Second World War ace, was shot down by flak during an attack on the rail yards at Kumu-ri and taken prisoner.

Other aces during 1952 included Lt. J. F. Low in June, Capt. C. D. Jolley in August, Capt. R. Risner and Maj. F. C. Blesse in September, and Col. Royal Baker, Lt. C. G. Forster, and Capt. L. W. Lilley in November. The last four months of 1952 found a number of MiGs being downed without actually being hit by gunfire. While taking evasive actions they would suddenly snap into spins accidentally and simply not be able to recover. In a few cases the pilots did manage to eject but most crashed with their aircraft.

The year 1953 saw sixteen more jet aces created; these were; Lt. H. E. Fischer, Capt. D. O. Overton, Capt. J. McConnell, Jr., Capt. J. P. Hagerstrom, Capt. J. K. Johnson, Lt.-Col. G. L. Jones, Lt.-Col. G. I. Ruddell, Lt.-Col. V. Garrison, Capt. L. R. Moore, Capt. R. S. Parr, Lt. H. Buttelmann, Capt. R. P. Baldwin, Capt. C. A. Curtain, Maj. S. L. Bettinger, Maj. J. F. Bolt, and Capt. M. J. Fernandez.

It is interesting to note that McConnell and Fernandez, two of the top three aces, scored most of their kills in the final months of the war. Other interesting extractions show Second World War aces duplicating their feat in Korea; Garrison, Hagerstrom and Bolt were the men who accomplished this trick. Bolt was a Marine pilot who served with the 51st Wing on an exchange basis. Another interesting note is that one of Lt. Buttelmann's kills saved the life of another Marine pilot, Major John Glenn, also an exchange pilot who in turn shot down a MiG that was on the tail of Buttelmann. The last kill of the war was scored by Capt. Parr on his last mission when he caught an Il-12 and shot it down just before the truce

Formation by the 1st Fighter Group, 27th Fighter Squadron. (USAF)

became effective. The Reds claim that it had been over neutral territory at the time.

While the most interesting career of any fighter is its combat life, the Sabre served in other vital capacities as well. The Sabre had a long lived career in the defense of the free world. It was a mainstay of the U.S.A.F.'s Air Defense Command for a number of years. When they were phased out of the regular air force many Sabres were passed on to the Air Guard units and continued to serve with them as a strong back up force.

The Sabre in Foreign Service

Under the Mutual Defense Assistance Program the United States provided a number of nations with various marks of the Sabre. A number were also manufactured by other nations, but these will be covered in a future AIRCAM, No. 20.

Fiat assembled F-86K's went to France, Italy and West Germany. A number of F-86K's were manufactured in the U.S. and sent to Norway and the Netherlands. Turkey received a dozen F-86F's. Spain received a number of F-86F-20's in exchange for the use of Spanish bases. The Italians received the YF-86K prototypes. Belgium was given five F-86F's and Portugal two.

South American countries acquired ex-U.S.A.F. surplus Sabres. Peru bought 14 F-86F-25's, Venezuela received six F-86F-30's and later got sixteen more. Argentina also purchased Sabres in 1961.

The Nationalist Chinese Air Force received a very large supply of Sabres, taking on charge many that had fought in Korea as well as newer models. In June of 1958 these Sabres once again tangled with Red Chinese MiG-15's and MiG-17's when they provided cover for the islands of Quemoy and Matsu; and again they got the best of the argument. Sabres ran up a score of 29 MiGs with no losses, and when Sidewinders were used they raised the first cry of brutality set up by the Reds. Korea and Japan were other Asiatic nations given Sabres by the United States, which also supplied the type to Pakistan, the Philippines, Thailand, and Iraq.

Any day now the last Sabre will finally be grounded and the saga will end; but it will be an epic saga, not easily matched by any jet fighter of the world's air forces.

Right: Last squadron of the 1st FG was the 71st Squadron, FU–633 seen here at the 1949 National Air Races. (W. T. Larkins)

Below: F–86A of the 27th Fighter Squadron, note the white outlined black squadron trim on this particular aircraft. (D. W. Menard)

Above: F–86A of the 'Silver Sabres' aerobatic team. Note two yellow stripes on tail-plane, white intake and outer-wing panels. (D. W. Menard)

Right: F–86A Sabre of the 146th Fighter Interceptor Wing, 115th Fighter Interceptor Squadron, California Air National Guard. Flown by Lt. John M. Conroy on 'Operation Boomerang' from Los Angeles to New York to Los Angeles, 5,085 miles in 11 hrs. 18 mins. 27 secs. on 21st May 1955. See colour illustration. (D. W. Menard)

Below: Same aircraft as above in later paint scheme, green nose and tank bands with red arrows. (D. W. Menard)

Above: 'Cindee Lind 6th', an F–86A of the Delaware Air National Guard. (D. W. Menard)

Above: 'Gal-O-My Dreams', an F–86A of the Oregon Air National Guard. Red/yellow/ white/red fuselage stripes outlined black, yellow/black fin and rudder band. (D. W. Menard)

Above: F–86A of the Utah Air National Guard, green trim with white and black outlining. All a/c letters in black. (D. W. Menard)

Below: F–86E of the Alaska Air National Guard, Note red nose, long-range tank and aft fuselage. (D. W. Menard)

Above: A pair of F–86E's of the 334th Fighter Squadron, 4th Fighter Wing taking off from a Korean airfield. FU–883 'Funfrus' flown by Lt. Col. William L. Crosby. Yellow outlined black fuselage, wing and tail bands. (USAF)

Left: Nice flying shot of a 336th Fighter Squadron Canadair built F–86E. (USAF)

Left: Line-up of F–86E's of the 336th Fighter Squadron, Chitose Air Base, Japan. (D. W. Menard)

Below: Line-up of F–86F's of the 8th Fighter Bomber Wing, unit converted from F–80's in April 1953. (USAF)

Above: 51st Fighter Interceptor Wing formation flying low over rugged Japanese countryside. (USAF)

Right: A sharkmouthed F–86F of the 51st Fighter Interceptor Wing, Tsuiki Air Base, Japan. 1954.

Below: Line-up of 8th Fighter Wing tail stripes. (USAF)

Above: F–86A 'Space Eater' of the 56th Fighter Group, O'Hare Air Force Base. See title page for colour details. (USAF)

Right: F–86E of the Arizona Air National Guard. See colour illustration. (D. W. Menard)

Below: F–86A of the 194th Fighter Interceptor Squadron, California Air National Guard, 'Old Leroy' of 'The Bald Eagles', colours unknown. (Norman E. Taylor)

Below: F–86F of the 435th Fighter Bomber Squadron at Detroit, Michigan, 1952. Red trim with white stars. (Norman E. Taylor)

Above: F–86F of Air Training Command, colour details are unknown. (D. W. Menard)

Right: Colourful F–86F of an unknown unit in Germany. Yellow nose, fuselage, wing and tail bands. (G. J. Letzter)

Below: F–86H taxying at Eglin Air Force Base, Florida. Insignia on fin is that of the Air Force Proving Ground; motto 'Proof by Trial'. (USAF)

Below: F–86H–5 with four 20mm M–39 guns. Eglin AFB, Florida. (USAF)

Above: F–86H of the 34th Fighter Squadron. (USAF)

Above & below: A pair of F–86H's of the New York Air National Guard, note 'The Boys From Syracuse' on the tank of O–31231. (Photos D. W. Menard)

Above: Starboard detail shot of a New York Air National Guard F–86H, note presentation of AFNG on upper surface of wing. (D. W. Menard)

Above: An F–86H of the DC Air National Guard, tail band red outlined black with white stars. (Gerhard Joos)

Right & below: Fore and aft views of an F–86H of the West Virginia Air National Guard. Red trim outlined white. (Photos D. W. Menard)

Above: Good detail shot of the starboard side of the nose of a DC Air National Guard F–86H–5. Serial 31329. (S. P. Peltz)

Right: 'Cindee Lind 9th', an F–86H of the Delaware Air National Guard. Yellow and black trim. (Gerhard Joos)

Below: Port side nose detail, F–86H of the Peurto Rico Air National Guard. Some of the Sabres of this unit were painted pale grey overall. Serial 31355. Yellow tail band with black outline. (S. P. Peltz)

Above: Line-up of F–86H's of the 101st Fighter Squadron, Massachusetts Air National Guard. Red fuselage stripes otherwise as colour illustration. Squadron Commander's aircraft. (D. W. Menard)

Right: F–86H, 101st Fighter Squadron, see colour illustration. (R. W. Harrison)

Below: Good detail shot of the starboard side of a 101st Fighter Squadron F–86H outside the squadron hangar. (D. W. Menard)

Right: F–86H of the 131st Fighter Squadron, Massachusetts Air National Guard with green and white Alaskan Exercise stripes, see colour illustration. (R. W. Harrison)

Below: F–86H of the Massachusetts Air National Guard in early scheme, see colour side views for nose and tail trim. (S. P. Peltz)

Above: Camouflaged F–86H of an unknown ANG unit, probably Maryland Air National Guard. (D. W. Menard)

Left: Detail shot showing starboard scheme. (Gerhard Joos)

Below: F–86H, 175th Tactical Fighter Group, Maryland Air National Guard. See colour illustration. (T. G. Handelman)

Below: Starboard side scheme detail shot, F–86H probably of the Maryland Air National Guard. (D. W. Menard)

Bottom: F–86H of the New York Air National Guard, note 'The Boys From Syracuse' in white on long-range tank. (D. W. Menard)

Above: F–86D of the 41st Fighter Interceptor Squadron. Red tail trim with black outline. (S. P. Peltz)

Below: Another F–86D of the 41st Fighter Interceptor Squadron, 'Miss Agnes', nose band and tail trim in red outlined black. (G. Cattaneo)

Below: F–86D of the 95th Fighter Interceptor Squadron, fuselage and tail stripes in red. (S. P. Peltz)

Below: F–86D of an unknown Fighter Interceptor Squadron. (D. W. Menard)

Above: F–86D of the 513th Fighter Interceptor Squadron, Phalsbourg Air Base, France. June 1959. Red fuselage flash with red and black tail trim. (D. W. Menard)

Above: F–86D of the 56th Fighter Interceptor Wing taxying along runway at O'Hare Air Force Base, May 1955. (D. W. Menard)

Below: Colourful F–86D of an unknown unit at the 1953 National Air Show. Fuselage trim and 97 in red with black details. (William T. Larkins)

Below: F–86D of the 'Sabre Knights' Aerobatic Team. See colour illustration. (D. W. Menard)

Above: Very nice flying shot of an F–86L, note SAGE antenna below fuselage. All F–86L's were modified F–86D–10 to –60 aircraft. (USAF)

Left: F–86D of the 465th Fighter Interceptor Squadron taking off from McChord Air Force Base, Washington, 1953. Red lightning flashes on tail. (Norman E. Taylor)

Below: Colourful F–86D flown by Lt. Edward G. Schultz of the 37th Fighter Interceptor Group. Blue nose and tail band with white stars, red aft fuselage and tail, note high position of serial on fin, 16065. (E. R. McDowell)

Below: F–86D of the California Air National Guard, note ANG insignia on fin otherwise standard USAF scheme. (D. W. Menard)

Above & below: Spick and span F–86D of the New Hampshire Air National Guard prior to the introduction of the day-glo panels as illustrated in the photograph below. Tail band and tank nose are green outlined black, see colour illustration. 3593 modified to F–86L standard. (Photos D. W. Menard)

Left: F–86D of the California Air National Guard, dark areas indicate day-glo high-visibility paint. (Gerhard Joos)

Right & below: A pair of F–86D's of the Illinois Air National Guard in early and late lettering schemes. (Photos D. W. Menard)

Above: 'Ruth I', a No. 2 'Flying Cheetah' Squadron, SAAF F–86F flying in formation with a Royal Navy Sea Fury. Note squadron insignia, black B and serial 603, otherwise as colour illustration. (SAAF)

Above: 613 well covered against the bitter Korean winter. An F–86F of No. 2 SAAF on Kimpoh airfield. (SAAF)

Below: 'Ruth I' running up in its dispersal area on a Korean airfield. (USAF)

Below: A trio of No. 2 Squadron Sabres taxying out to the runway prior to take-off on a combined mission with Sabres of the 18th FBW. From left to right; 'Imp VIII', 'She' and 'Just Joan'. See colour illustrations for No. 2 Squadron and 18th FBW Sabres. (USAF)

Left: F–86F of No. 332 Squadron Royal Norwegian Air Force, code AH–. Note presentation of squadron badge on blue shield in silver and blue.

Nice shot of a No. 331 Squadron Sabre, Royal Norwegian Air Force. Black trim on nose and lightning flash, red, white and blue flash on fin. (S. P. Peltz)

Left F–86F of No. 336 Squadron, red, white and blue nose bands, red flash on fuselage. Note squadron badge, a diving swallow on fin. (D. W. Menard)

Below: Another F–86F of No. 336 Squadron, colours as above. A Unit Insignia sheet will shortly be published on the Royal Norwegian Air Force. (S. P. Peltz)

A

1
F–86A Sabre of the 'Silver Sabres' Aerobatic Team, 4th Fighter Group, 335th Fighter Squadron.

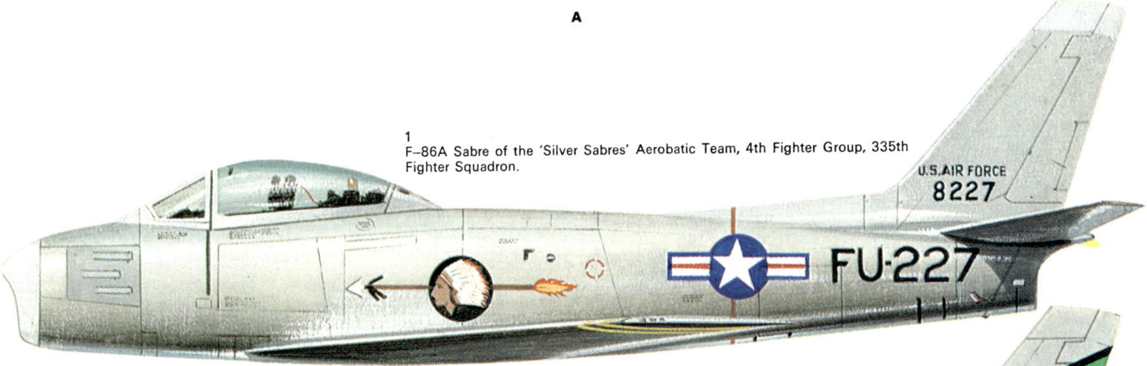

2
F–86A Sabre, 146th Fighter Interceptor Wing, 115th Fighter Interceptor Squadron, California Air National Guard. 'California Boomerang.'

3
F–86E Sabre, 51st Fighter Interceptor Wing, 5th Air Force, Korea. May 1953. Canadair built.

4
F–86E Sabre, Alaska Air National Guard. Elmendorf Field, Alaska. 1955.

5
F–86E Sabre, Arizona Air National Guard.

B

1
F–86F Sabre, 18th Fighter-Bomber Wing, 67th Fighter-Bomber Squadron, Kadena AFB, Okinawa.

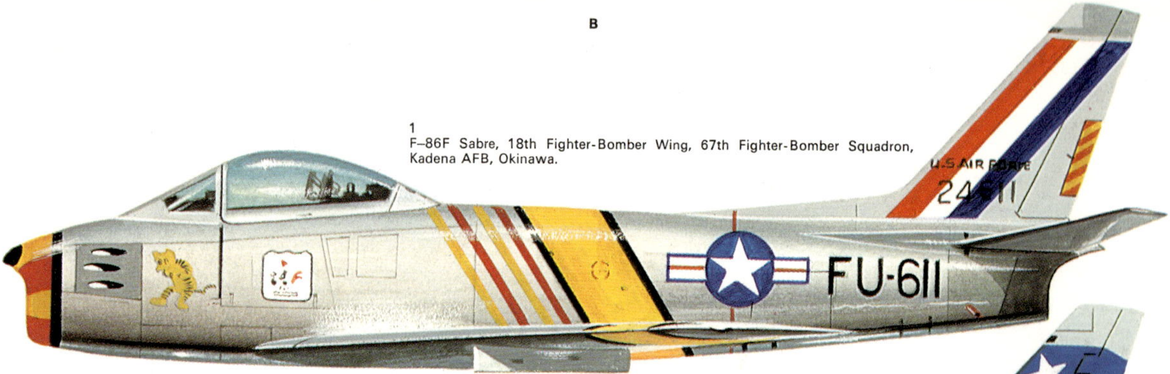

2
F–86E Sabre of the 'Skyblazers' Aerobatic Team.

3
F–86F Sabre, No. 2 'Flying Cheetahs' Fighter Squadron, South African Air Force, Korea, 1953.

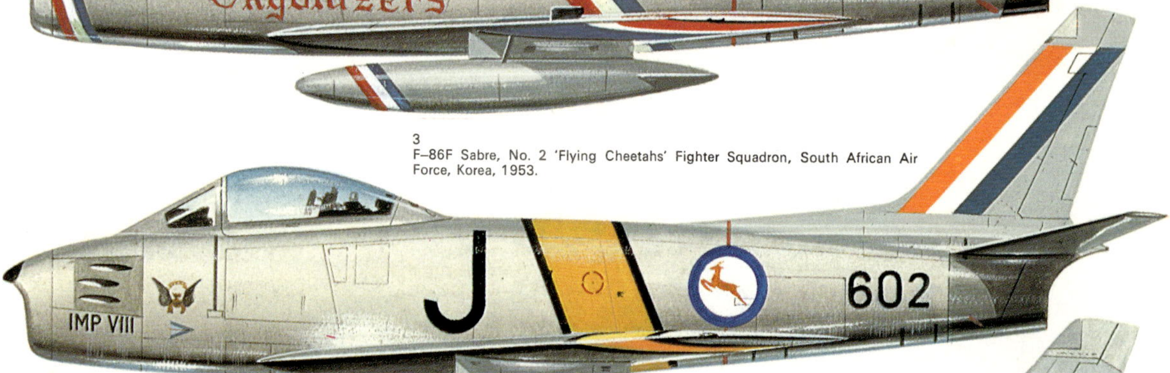

4
F–86F Sabre, No. 336 Fighter Squadron, Royal Norwegian Air Force.

5
F–86F Sabre, No. 338 Fighter Squadron, Royal Norwegian Air Force.

© WARD

1
F–86D Sabre, 53rd Fighter Interceptor Wing, 14th Fighter Interceptor Squadron, USAF.

2
F–86L Sabre, 133rd Fighter Interceptor Squadron, New Hampshire Air National Guard. Grenier Air Force Base, N.H. 1959.

3
F–86D Sabre, 440th Fighter Interceptor Squadron, USAF.

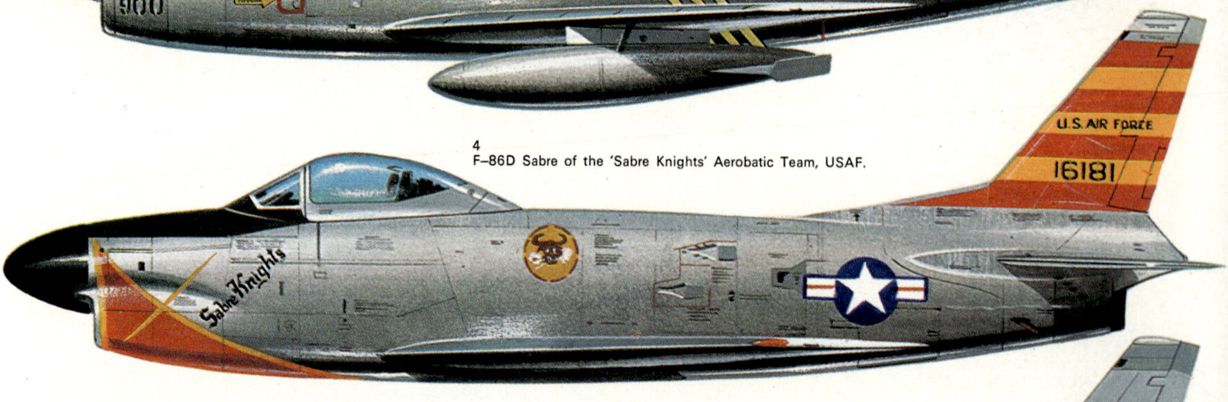

4
F–86D Sabre of the 'Sabre Knights' Aerobatic Team, USAF.

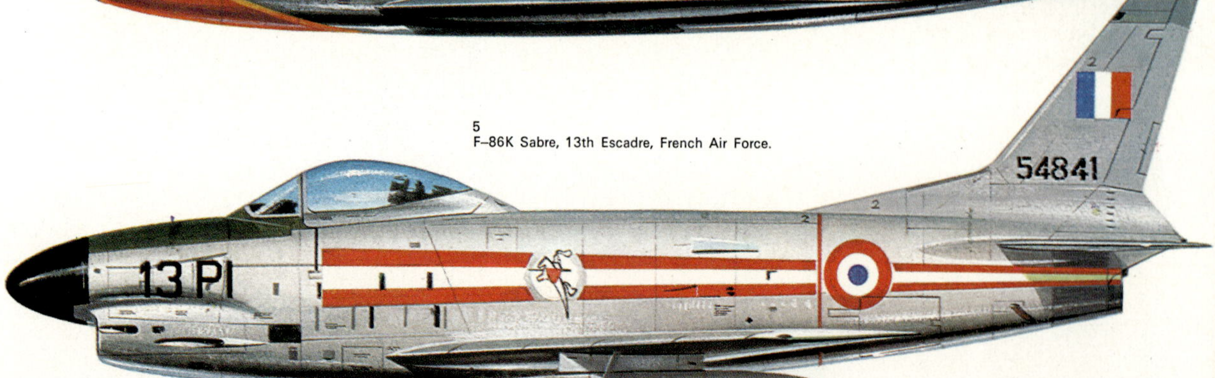

5
F–86K Sabre, 13th Escadre, French Air Force.

Published by ARCO PUBLISHING COMPANY, INC., 219 Park Avenue South, N.Y., N.Y. 10003. Printed in Great Britain.

c

1
F–86F Sabre, No. 1 Fighter Interceptor Group, Portuguese Air Force.

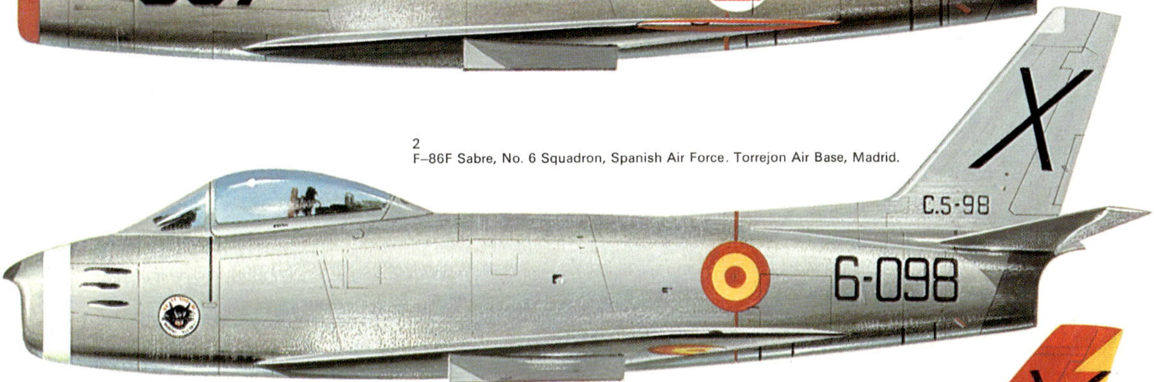

2
F–86F Sabre, No. 6 Squadron, Spanish Air Force. Torrejon Air Base, Madrid.

3
F–86F Sabre, No. 1 Squadron, Spanish Air Force Aerobatic Team.

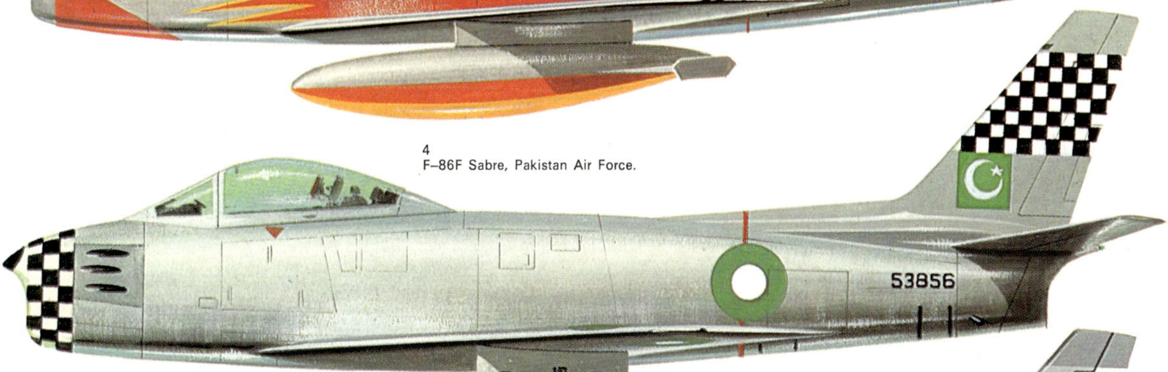

4
F–86F Sabre, Pakistan Air Force.

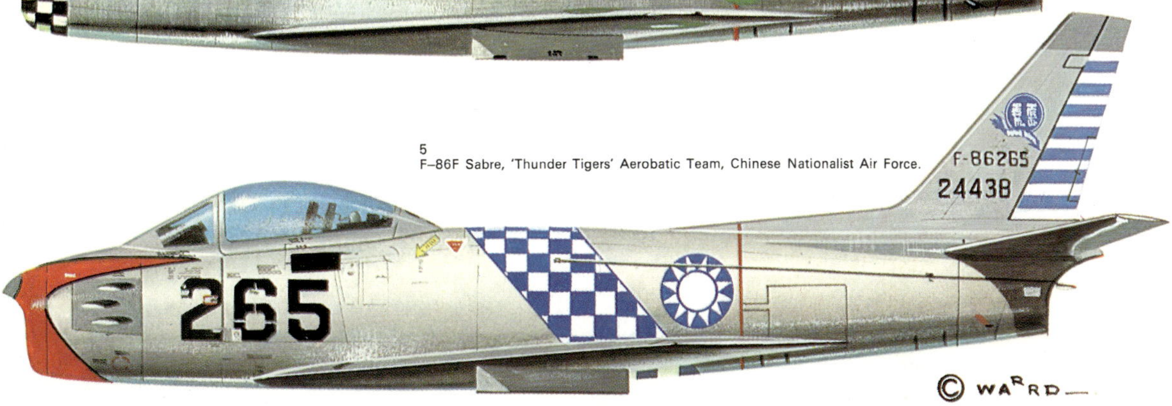

5
F–86F Sabre, 'Thunder Tigers' Aerobatic Team, Chinese Nationalist Air Force.

D

1
F–86F Sabre, Argentine Air Force.

2
F–86F Sabre, Venezuelan Air Force.

3
F–86F Sabre, No. 12 Group, Peruvian Air Force.

4
RF–86F Sabre, Republic of Korea Air Force.

5
F–86F Sabre, 'Blue Diamonds' Aerobatic Team, Philippine Air Force.

E

1
F–86F Sabre, 1st Wing, 1st Squadron, Japanese Air Self Defence Force.

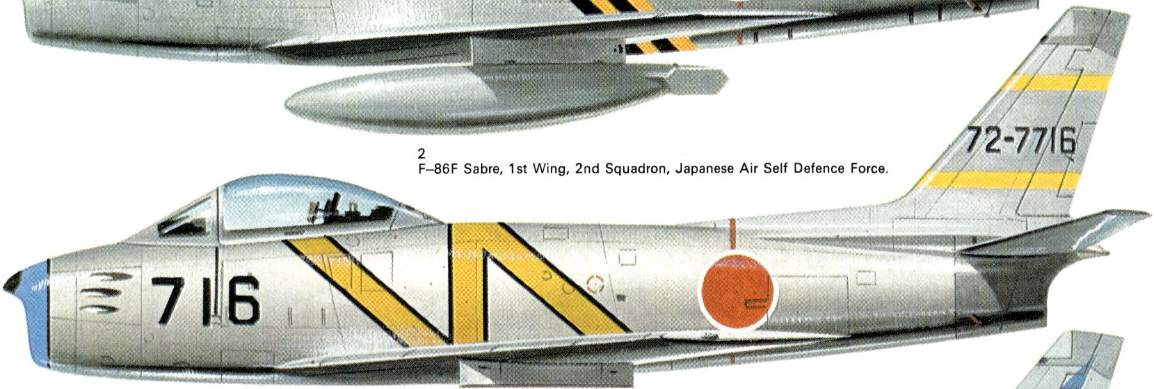

2
F–86F Sabre, 1st Wing, 2nd Squadron, Japanese Air Self Defence Force.

3
RF–86F Sabre, 501st Tactical Reconnaissance Squadron, Japanese Air Self Defence Force.

4
F–86F Sabre, 'Blue Impulse' Aerobatic Team, Team Leader's aircraft. Japanese Air Self Defence Force.

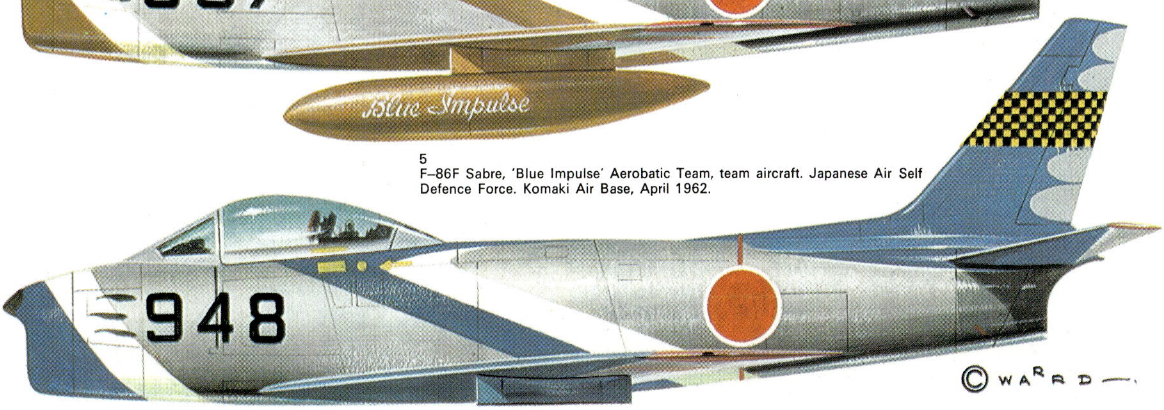

5
F–86F Sabre, 'Blue Impulse' Aerobatic Team, team aircraft. Japanese Air Self Defence Force. Komaki Air Base, April 1962.

F

1
F–86F Sabre, Royal Thai Air Force.

2
F–86H Sabre, 101st Tactical Fighter Squadron, 104th Tactical Fighter Group, Massachusetts Air National Guard.

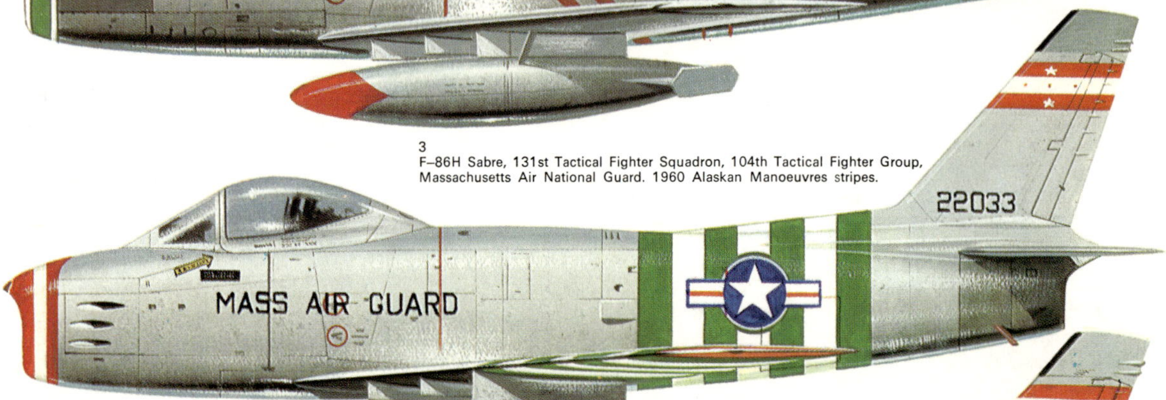

3
F–86H Sabre, 131st Tactical Fighter Squadron, 104th Tactical Fighter Group, Massachusetts Air National Guard. 1960 Alaskan Manoeuvres stripes.

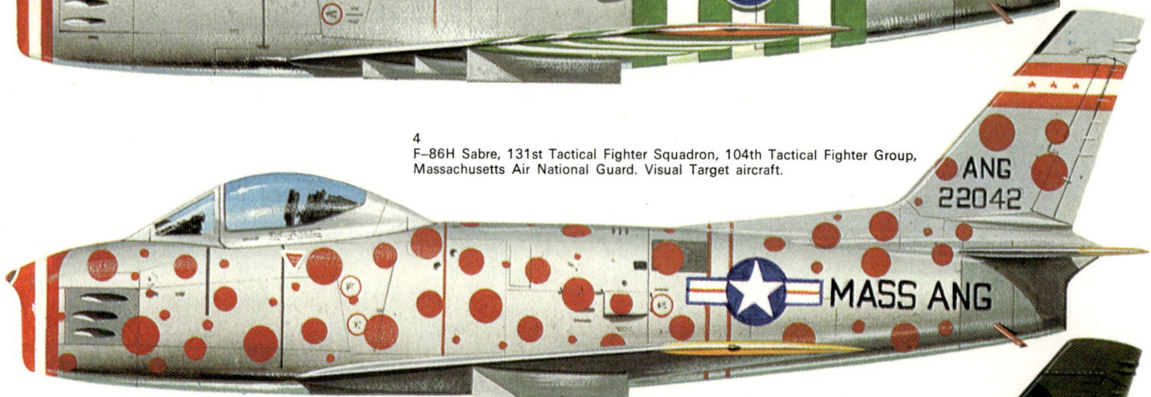

4
F–86H Sabre, 131st Tactical Fighter Squadron, 104th Tactical Fighter Group, Massachusetts Air National Guard. Visual Target aircraft.

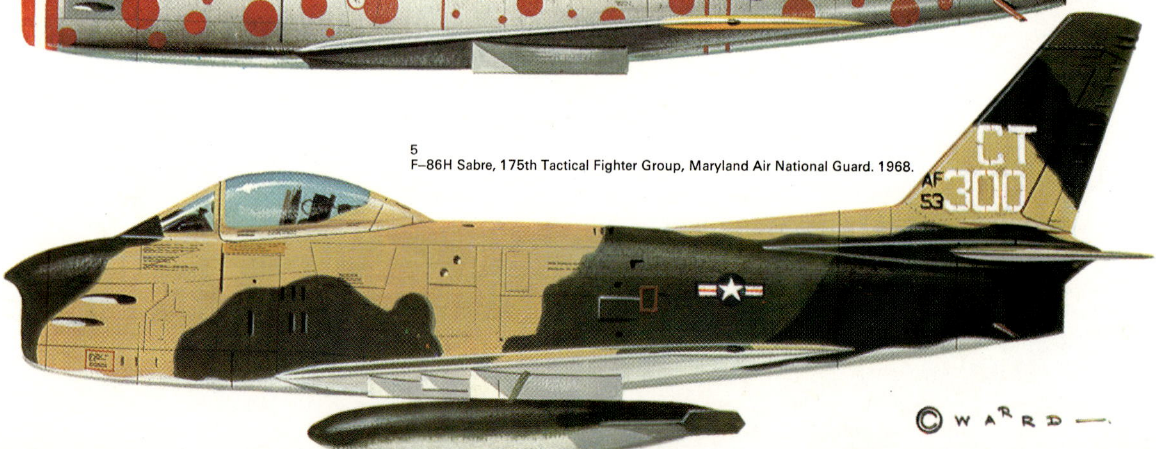

5
F–86H Sabre, 175th Tactical Fighter Group, Maryland Air National Guard. 1968.

G

1
F–86K Sabre, No. 700 Squadron, Royal Netherlands Air Force.

2
F–86K Sabre, No. 334 Squadron, Royal Norwegian Air Force.

3
F–86D Sabre, No. 726 Squadron, Royal Danish Air Force.

4
F–86K Sabre, 51st Aerobrigata, Italian Air Force.

5
F–86K Sabre, Jagdgeschwader 74, West German Luftwaffe.

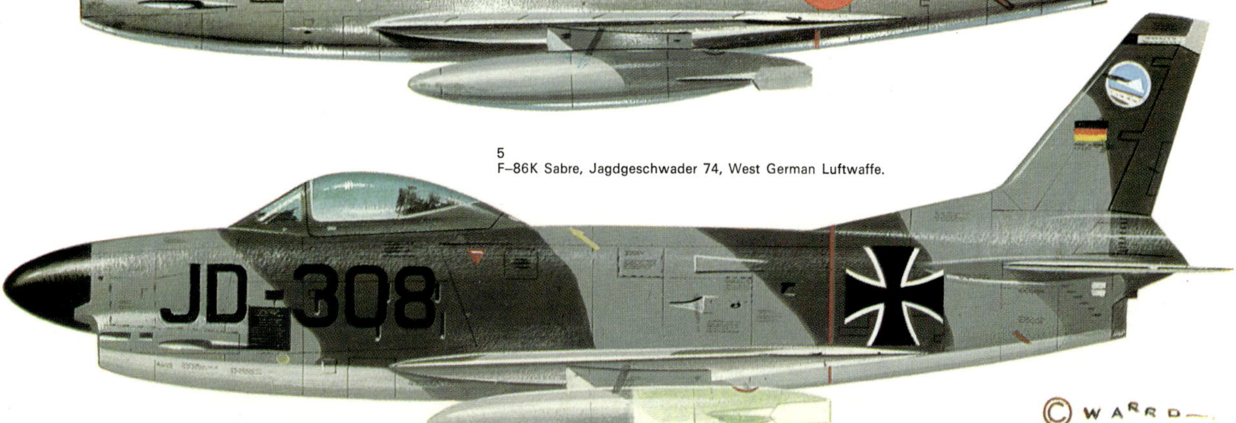

H

1
F–86D Sabre, Yugoslav Air Force.

2
F–86D Sabre, Philippine Air Force.

3
F–86D Sabre, 3rd Wing, 105th Squadron, Japanese Air Self Defence Force.

4
F–86D Sabre, Republic of Korea Air Force.

5
F–86D Sabre, Royal Thai Air Force.

Above: Nice flying shot of a No. 338 Squadron F–86F over rugged Norwegian countryside. Tail colours are black/yellow/black. (Royal Norwegian Air Force)

Above: Another No. 338 Squadron F–86F, note later code presentation where the aircraft was indicated by a number and not as previously a letter. (S. P. Peltz)

Above: F–86K of No. 332 Squadron, R.Norw.AF. Note a/c letter on fin and overpainted squadron badge, pale green radar dome. (S. P. Peltz)

Below: Sharkmouth F–86K of No. 337 Squadron, see AIRCAM SPECIAL SHARKMOUTH for colour illustration. (S. P. Peltz)

Above: F–86K of an unknown unit, Royal Norwegian Air Force.

Above: Another Sharkmouthed Sabre of No. 337 Squadron. Note squadron badge, a sword superimposed on a clover leaf on the fin. (via G. Cattanec

Below left: F–86K of No. 337 Squadron, note code change from ZK–. Very pale green radome, black/red mouth with blue lips (S. P. Peltz)

Below right: F–86K of No. 339 Squadron, see front cover for colour details. (S. P. Peltz)

Below: F–86K of Jagdgeschwader JG74 showing the starboard side camouflage presentation, code is JD 320 in black. All F–86K's illustrated are from JG74. (S. P. Peltz)

Above: JD 334 streaming its braking chute during landing run at its home base, in this instance the chute is all white. (S. P. Peltz)

Below: JD 308 showing standard Luftwaffe camouflage scheme, note in all cases the aft end of tanks are white. (S. P. Peltz)

Above: F–86K of the 1st Aerobrigata, Italian Air Force. Note serial on fin in stencil characters and 1st Aerobrigata insignia on green band. (Italian Air Force)

Below: F–86K of the 51st Aerobrigata, Italian Air Force, serial 38300. Note 51st insignia on red tail band. (G. Cattaneo)

Above: Nice break by Sabres of No. 700 Squadron, Royal Netherlands Air Force, note the formal presentation of the squadron insignia on the fin of Q–255. (Royal Netherlands Air Force)

Above: Nice flying shot of a F–86K of the Royal Netherlands Air Force, note early presentation of fin flash with USAF serial 54–1278 above and Royal Netherlands Air Force serial Q–278 below in small black lettering. (Royal Netherlands Air Force)

Below: Good rear end flying view of Q–310, note position of wing and fuselage roundel. No. 700 Squadron, Royal Netherlands Air Force. (Royal Netherlands Air Force)

Above: Good detail shot of a No. 700 Squadron F–86K. (S. P. Peltz)

Below: Ground shot of Q–310 taken at Hahn in May 1962. (D. W. Menard)

Below: Q–237 taxying along perimeter track prior to take-off, note presentation of No. 700 Squadron insignia on fin. USAF serial 54–1237 above insignia. (S. P. Peltz)

Above & below: Very nice flying shots of a F–86K of the 13th Escadre, French Air Force, see colour illustration. (French Air Force via J. Cuny)

Right: 13.QG serial 54822 being re-fuelled and re-armed at its home base Colmar. (D. W. Menard)

Below: 13.QQ serial 54850, note absence of insignia on fuselage. (French Air Force via J. Cuny)

Above: Nice shot of a 13th Escadre F–86K streaming its braking chute at Colmar. Chute is red. 13.QP serial 54849. (French Air Force via J. Cuny)

Below: Good detail shot of nose, note stencil markings around gun ports and olive drab anti-dazzle panel area typical to French aircraft only. (French Air Force via J. Cuny)

Right: A pair of F–86D's of the Yugoslav Air Force, see colour illustration.

Above & below: A colourful F–86D of No. 726 Squadron, Royal Danish Air Force, see colour illustration. (Jacob Støppel)

Left: F–86D of No. 726 Squadron in standard scheme. (D. W. Menard)

Below: This F–86D Sabre is the subject for the colour side-view, serial under fin flash is 16123 in black. (S. P. Peltz)

Above: Line-up of F–86F's of No. 1 Squadron, Spanish Air Force. Note the old Spanish Civil War era insignia with the motto 'Vista Suerte y al Toro', nose band is blue. Home base Manizes, Valencia. (D. W. Menard)

Left: F–86F of No. 4 Squadron, apparently with a white nose band though the allocated colour is green. Home base Son San Juan, Palma De Mallorca. (D. W. Menard)

Above: F–86F Sabre of No. 103 Fighter Bomber Squadron, red nose band otherwise standard natural metal scheme. (D. W. Menard)

Right & below: A pair of F–86F Sabres of No. 1 Fighter Interceptor Group, Portuguese Air Force. See colour illustration. (Photos D. W. Menard)

Above: Line-up of F–86F's of the 1st Wing, 1st Squadron, Japanese Air Self Defence Force. These are USAF supplied aircraft used primarily for the training of Japanese air and ground crews prior to the Mitsubishi built Sabres being issued to units. (USAF)

Left: F–86F of the 5th Wing, tail bands and nose band in red. (D. W. Menard)

Above: Line-up of F–86F's of 4th Wing, 5th Squadron, insignia on fin and rudder red. (G. C. Voldonio)

Left: Line-up of 7th Wing, 9th Squadron Sabres, insignia is blue with black shadow. Missawa Air Base, May 1964. (D. W. Menard)

Above & right: RF–86F's of 501st Tac Recon Squadron, see colour illustration. (Photos above via G. Cattaneo, right D. W. Menard)

Below left: F–86F of the 82nd Squadron, Iwakuni AB. (S. P. Peltz)

Below right: F–86F of a Headquarter Flight, insignia is red, yellow and blue. (S. P. Peltz)

Above: Line-up of the present day 'Blue Impulse' Aerobatic Team, see front cover illustration. (T. Shibusawa)

Below: F–86D of the 2nd Wing, 103rd Squadron, tail bands are pale blue with white outline (D. W. Menard)

Above: Line-up of F–86F Sabres of the Royal Thai Air Force. See side-view illustration for colour details. (D. W. Menard)

Left: Interesting shot of a Sabre slowing down towards the end of its landing run, note red outlined no step area inboard on each flap. (R. A. Brown)

Right: 5000 taxying to its dispersal area, note leaping tiger insignia on nose. (R. A. Brown)

Above: F–86F rolling down the runway at Bangkok, for colour details see the F–86D side-view illustration. (R. A. Brown)

Left: A pair of F–86D Sabres of the all-weather interceptor squadron, these aircraft replaced F–86F's. (D. W. Menard)

Above: ROK F–86F's dispersed in bomb-blast pens, serials from left to right are; 25349, 24656 and 113192. (USAF)

Right: RF–86F of the ROK Air Force, see side-view for colour details. (D. W. Menard)

Above: ROKAF F–86F, note four long-range tanks and stencil style of lettering. See front cover for colour details. (S. P. Peltz)

Right: F–86D fully armed waiting on its dispersal area ready to scramble. Note R.O.K. Air Force on fin is in OD not black. See colour illustration. (D. W. Menard)

Below: F–86F of the Chinese Nationalist Air Force 'Thunder Tigers' Aerobatic Team, see colour illustration. (S. P. Peltz)

Above: Philippine Air Force F–86F's, nearest aircraft is the squadron commander's. Note blue, red and yellow bands separated by white on tail and fuselage. (S. P. Peltz)

Below: F–86F of the 'Blue Diamonds' Aerobatic Team, see side-view illustration. (D. W. Menard)

Left: Philippine F–86F in standard natural metal scheme. (D. W. Menard)

Below: F–86D Sabre of the Philippine Air Force, see colour illustration. (D. W. Menard)

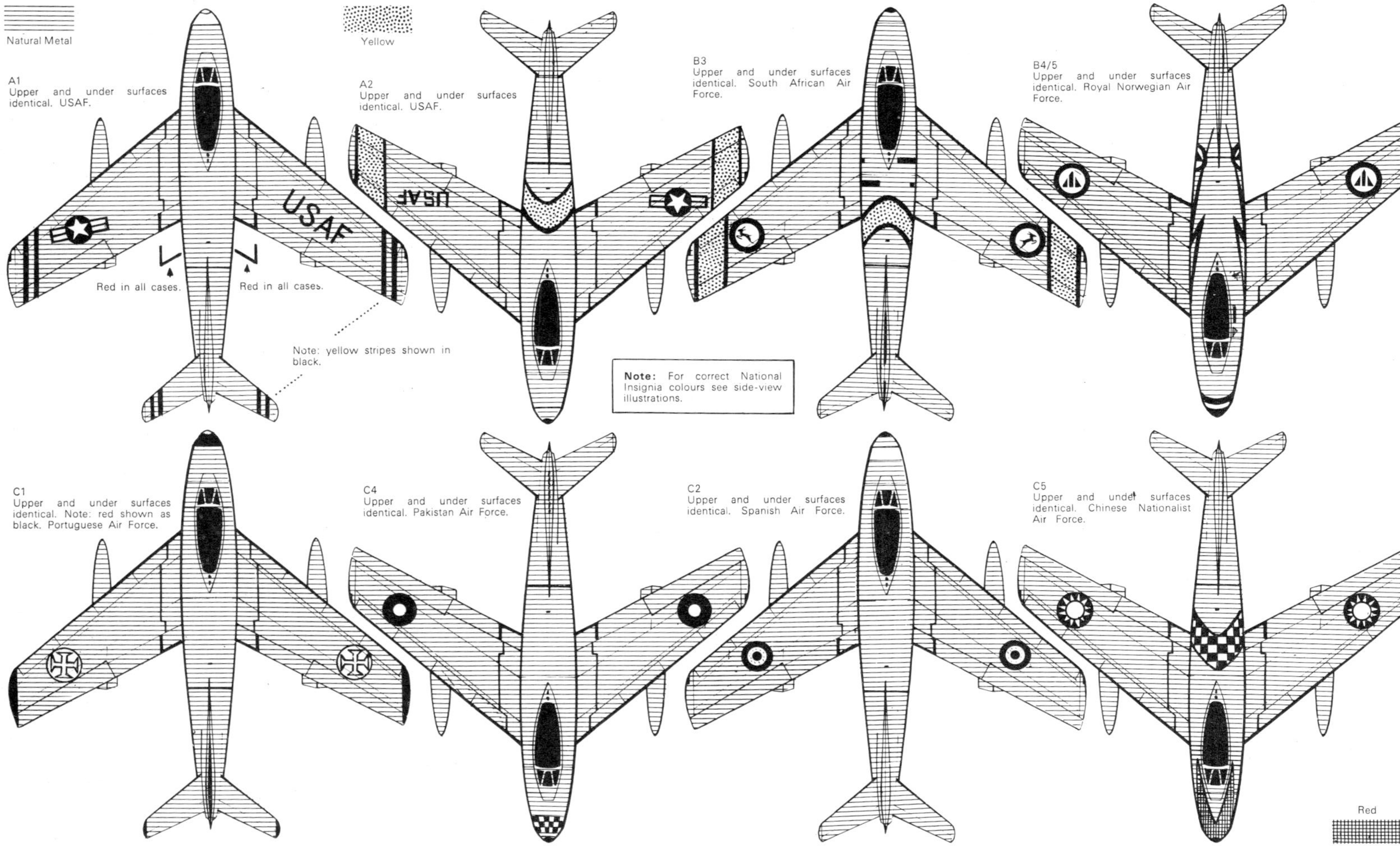
Natural Metal
Yellow
A1
Upper and under surfaces identical. USAF.
USAF
Red in all cases.
Red in all cases.
Note: yellow stripes shown in black.
A2
Upper and under surfaces identical. USAF.
USAF
B3
Upper and under surfaces identical. South African Air Force.
B4/5
Upper and under surfaces identical. Royal Norwegian Air Force.
Note: For correct National Insignia colours see side-view illustrations.
C1
Upper and under surfaces identical. Note: red shown as black. Portuguese Air Force.
C4
Upper and under surfaces identical. Pakistan Air Force.
C2
Upper and under surfaces identical. Spanish Air Force.
C5
Upper and under surfaces identical. Chinese Nationalist Air Force.
Red

Natural Metal

D4
Upper and under surfaces identical. USAF style. Republic of Korea Air Force.

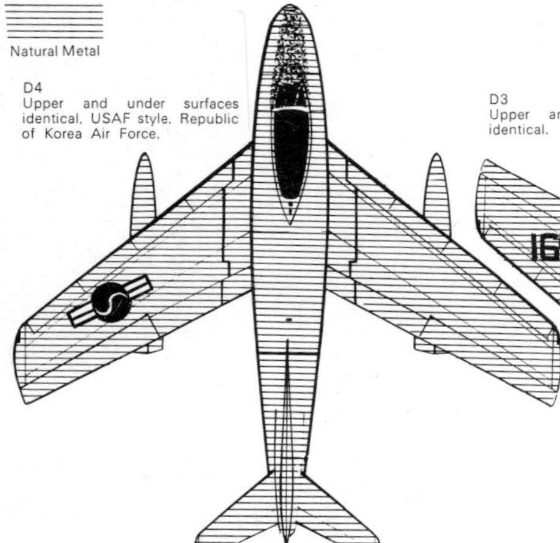

D3
Upper and under surfaces identical. Peruvian Air Force.

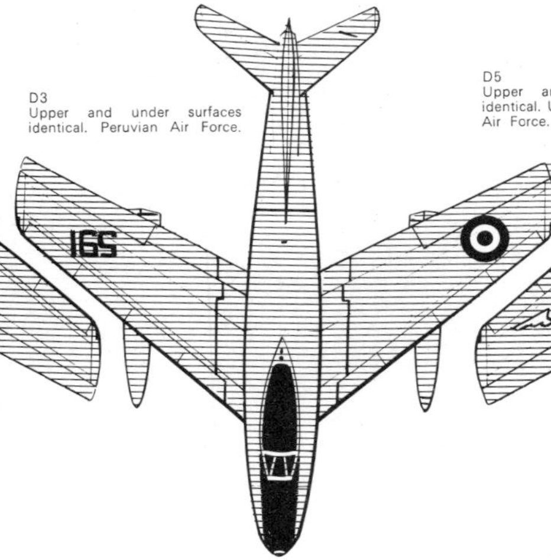

D5
Upper and under surfaces identical. USAF style. Philippine Air Force.

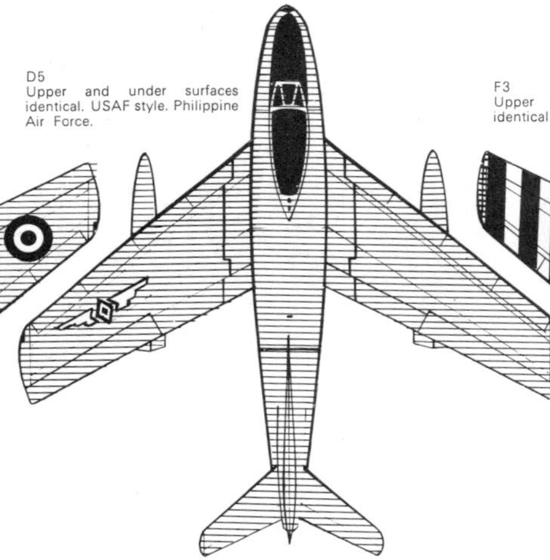

F3
Upper and under surfaces identical. USAF.

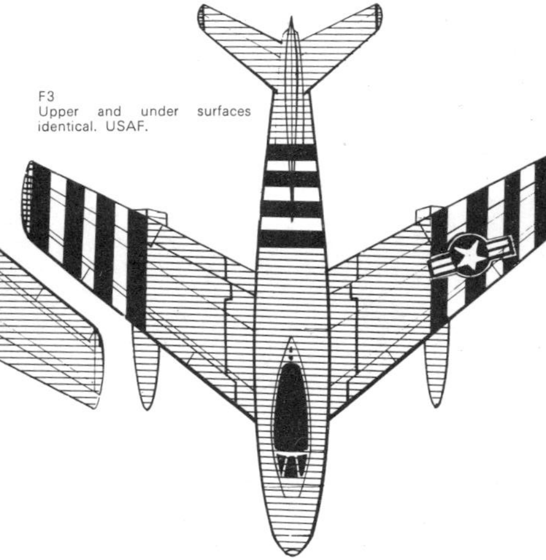

E6
Upper surface only.
Note: Black indicates medium blue except for roundels. 'Blue Impulse' JASDF Aerobatic Team.

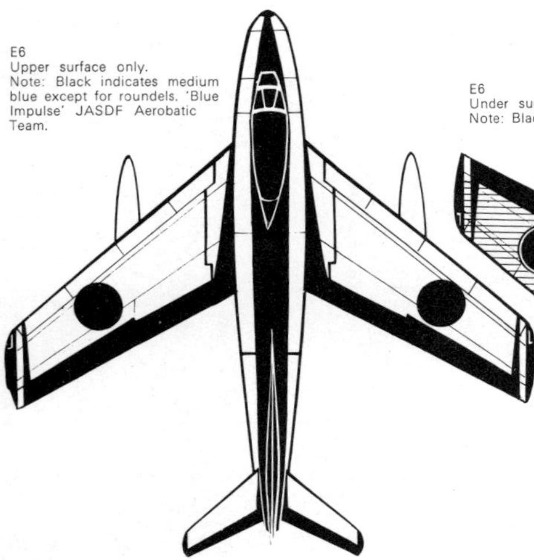

E6
Under surface only.
Note: Black indicates red.

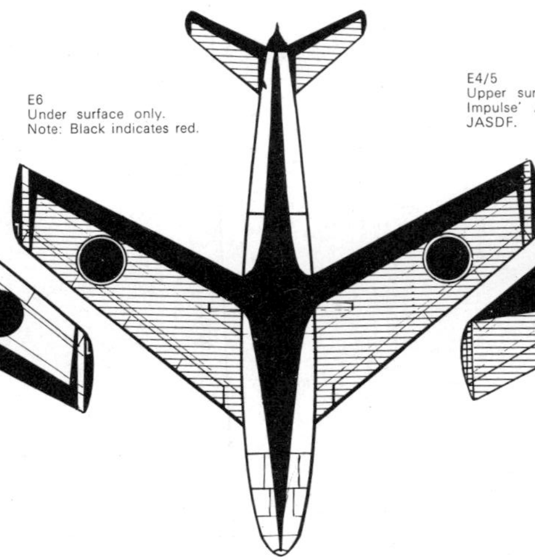

E4/5
Upper surface scheme. 'Blue Impulse' Aerobatic Team, JASDF.

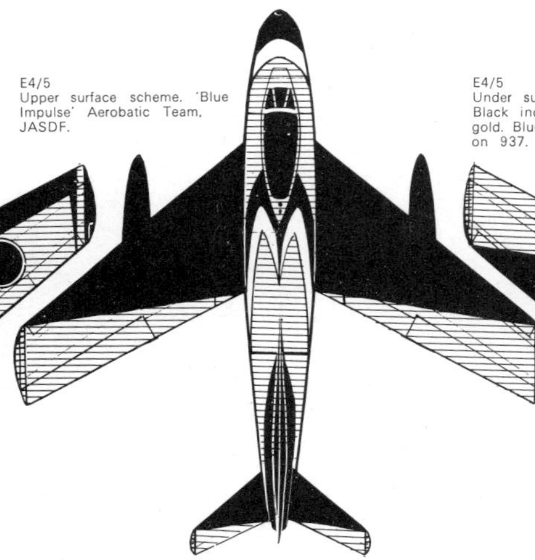

E4/5
Under surface scheme. Note: Black indicates dark blue or gold. Blue tanks on 948, gold on 937.

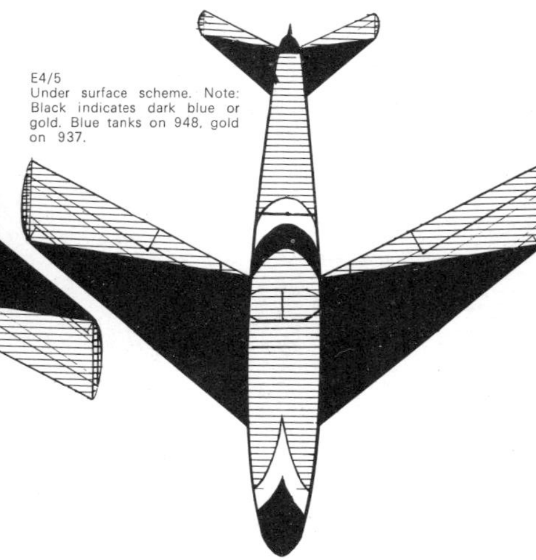